W9-CAR-479

FORTVILLE VERNON - TWP PUBLIC LIBRARY
625 EAST BROADWAY
FORTVILLE, IN 46040

DEMCO

FORTVILLE PUBLIC LIBRARY
FORTVILLE, INDIANA 46040

A New True Book

AIRPORTS

By David Petersen

This "true book" was prepared
under the direction of
Illa Podendorf,
formerly with the Laboratory School,
University of Chicago

CHILDRENS PRESS, CHICAGO

PHOTO CREDITS
Federal Aviation Administration, Great Lakes
Public Affairs Office—cover, 2, 4, 6, 8, 12
(3 photos), 14 (2 photos), 16 (2 photos), 21
(2 photos), 23, 24 (2 photos), 27, 28, 30, 31, 34,
40 (2 photos), 42
(top and middle pictures), 44,
45 (2 photos)
Cosette Winter—10
James P. Rowan—18
American Airlines—33, 38 (2 photos), 42 (bottom)
United Press International—25
Tony Freeman—36

Library of Congress Cataloging in Publication Data

Peterson, David.
  Airports.

  (A New true book)
  SUMMARY: Briefly discusses the history and
kinds of airports, the various activities in a
large airport, and what happens during a trip
on an airplane.
  1. Airports—Juvenile literature.
[1. Airports.   2. Aeronautics, Commercial]
I. Title.
TL725.P44   387.7'36   81-7736
ISBN 0-516-01607-5   AACR2

Copyright© 1981 by Regensteiner Publishing Enterprises, Inc.
All rights reserved. Published simultaneously in Canada.
Printed in the United States of America.
  2 3 4 5 6 7 8 9 10 R 90 89 88 87 86 85 84 83 82

TABLE OF CONTENTS

Runways at least two miles long are needed by large airplanes.

WHAT ARE AIRPORTS?

Airports are special places for airplanes. Airports have many services to help airplane pilots and passengers.

Some airports are very small. Sometimes just a farmer's field or a dirt road is an "airport."

Only small airplanes can use small airports. Bigger airplanes need the services of large airports. They need long runways.

Taxiways connect runways at large airports.

THE RUNWAY

A runway is like a smooth and level road. Airplanes need runways to take off.

An airplane has to be going fast down the runway to take off. Some go almost 150 miles per hour before they take off.

Lights help pilots find and land on runways.

Some runways have lights down their sides and middle. These lights help pilots see at night and in bad weather.

WIND SOCKS

Most airports have a wind sock. The wind sock is at the top of a pole. When the wind blows, it fills the wind sock up. Wind socks show from which direction the wind is blowing and how hard.

The wind's direction and speed are very important to pilots. Airplanes usually take off and land into the wind.

Even a home-built airplane that uses a very small field needs a wind sock.

THE CONTROL TOWER

A large airport has a control tower. The tower is usually a tall, round building. There are windows around the top. People work here. They are called air traffic controllers.

Control towers are taller than the other buildings at an airport.

Air traffic controllers in the control tower keep airplane traffic in order.

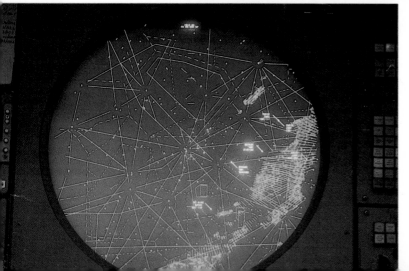

Radar scopes show where all the airplanes in a certain area are.

The controllers can see all of the airport from the tower. They watch all the airplanes, the runways, and the passenger buildings.

Other controllers make sure one airplane doesn't get in the way of another. They use radar scopes and radios to keep track of airplanes.

Airplanes can be fixed or stored in the large buildings called hangars.

HANGARS

Many airports have special buildings for airplanes. These are called hangars.

Airplanes can be put inside hangars. There they are worked on. The hangars can also keep airplanes safe from bad weather.

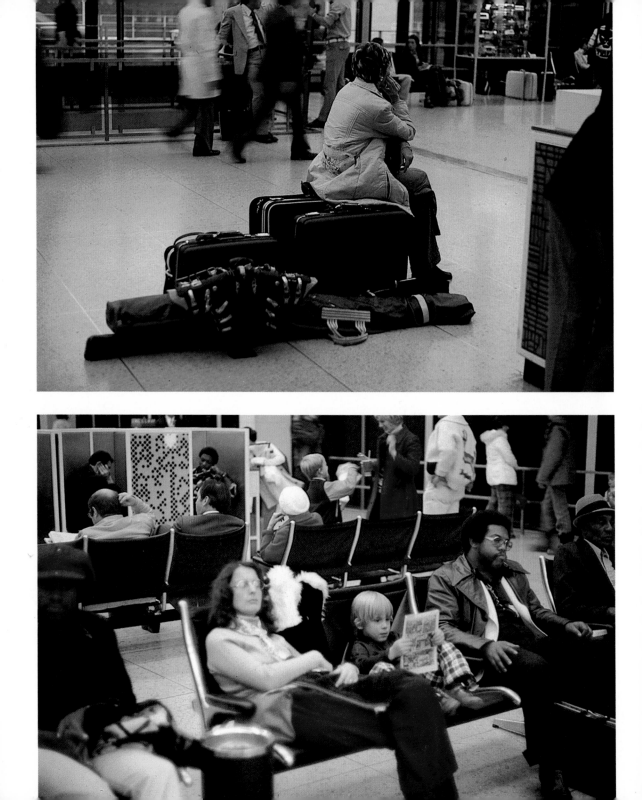

THE TERMINAL

All large airports have buildings called passenger terminals.

People wait in the terminals to get on airplanes. People can also wait there for others who are coming by airplane.

18

AIRLINERS

Most people fly on large
jets called airliners.
Airliners are made for
carrying many people at
one time. Some airliners
can carry 400 people!

In the early 1900s the first airplane flew. By the 1920s airplanes carried passengers. But there weren't many airliners. In 1926 there were only 26 in all of the United States.

Today airplanes are very important for carrying people and cargo. There are thousands of airliners now. They carry about 280 million people every year.

OTHER KINDS OF AIRPORTS

Some kinds of aircraft don't need airports. Others have their own special airports.

Helicopters can take off and land without a runway. Special airports for helicopters are called heliports.

At the heliport are
several large concrete
"pads." Helicopters take off
and land from these
helipads.

Hot-air balloons   Blimp

Blimps and hot-air
balloons don't need
runways, either. But they
do need lots of room. They
are very big. They often
use large fields as
"airports."

Aircraft carrier

Some airplanes take off and land on the decks of large ships. These floating airports are called aircraft carriers. Carriers are a little like airports. Runways are painted on their decks. The ships have control towers.

AN AIRLINE TRIP

What could passengers see on an airplane trip?

When they get to the terminal, passengers go to a ticket counter. Here they can buy tickets and check in. They can turn in their bags.

The person behind the counter checks in the bags. A pilot must know how much luggage is going on each flight. Then the airplane won't be overloaded.

The bags are then put on a moving belt. They are taken out to the airliner. They are put in the bottom of the airplane.

A metal detector gate

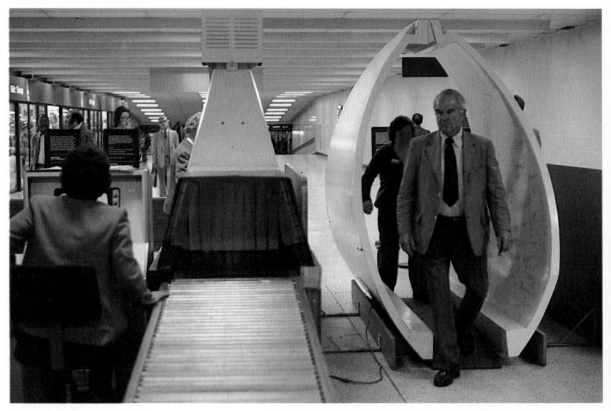

Next, passengers walk to a gate area. On the way there is a special area. Everyone must be checked here. There is a noise if someone carries metal through it. Keys could make a noise. So could a weapon. No weapons on an airplane make a safer ride for everyone.

The loading gate is attached to the side door of an airliner.

In the gate area people can sit until their airplane is ready. Or they can watch airplanes take off and land.

At last the airplane is ready for passengers. The passengers walk to the loading gate.

ON THE AIRPLANE

Inside, the airplane has long aisles and rows of seats.

Each seat has a number. The passengers' tickets tell them which seat to use.

The pilot checks his plane. When everyone is seated, the flight attendants look around. They make sure safety belts are fastened. The safety belts are like seat belts in cars.

The flight attendants tell the pilot that everyone is ready. The pilot starts the airplane's engines.

The pilot and copilot

The airplane taxis
slowly to the runway.
When the airplane is in its
takeoff position, the pilot
radios the control tower.
He asks for permission to
take off.

The pilot checks his airplane again. Then he gives the airplane full power.

The airplane starts to roll down the runway. It goes faster and faster. The passengers feel themselves being pushed back in the seats.

Jet engines give an airplane the power to climb into the air.

When the airplane is going fast enough, the pilot pulls back on his steering yoke. The yoke controls the airplane. The airplane then climbs into the air.

The pilot keeps the airplane climbing. The control tower tells him how high to go. The passengers by the windows can see the airport below. It looks smaller and smaller.

People can read, rest, and have a meal aboard an airliner.

THE LANDING

The flight can be
minutes or hours long. But
soon it is time to land. The
pilot radios the airport for
a landing okay. The control
tower tells the pilot when
it is time to land. The pilot
pushes forward on the
yoke. The airplane begins
to go lower.

A pilot's look at an airport.

The wheels, or landing gear, must be down and locked into place before the airplane can land.

FORTVILLE PUBLIC LIBRARY
FORTVILLE, INDIANA 46040

The airplane touches the runway. The tires make a loud screeching noise. The pilot brakes once the airplane is down.

Some airports roll
steps up to the side
door of an airplane.

Others use a loading
gate for passengers
to walk through.

Baggage is checked
to see that it is
in the right place.

The pilot takes the airplane down a taxiway. He then pulls the airplane up to the passenger terminal.

The flight attendants open the door. Passengers get off and go into the terminal. They walk to the baggage claim area. Here the bags are brought in on another moving belt.

People get their bags and
can leave the airport.

Airports are busy and
important places. A trip to
the airport can be fun.

WORDS YOU SHOULD KNOW

aircraft carrier (AYR • kraft KAYR • ee • er) — a very large ship that carries aircraft that can land and leave from its deck.

air traffic controller (AYR TRAF • ik kun • TROLL • er) — a person who helps pilots take off and land the aircraft

bag — suitcase; luggage

baggage claim area (BAG • aj CLAYM AYR • ee • uh) — the part of an airport where passengers can get their suitcases

blimp — a large balloon that can carry people and cargo

concrete (KON • kreet) — a building material made of sand, water, cement, and pebbles

control tower (kun • TROLL TOW • er) — a high room where workers can help aircraft land and take off

deck — the floor of a boat or ship

flight attendant (FLYT uh • TEN • dunt) — a person who works on an airplane and serves passengers

goods — things that can be bought and sold

hangar (HANG • er) — a large building where aircraft can be placed

helicopter (HEL • ih • kop • ter) — an aircraft without wings

helipad (HEL • ih • pad) — a spot where a helicopter can land

heliport (HEL • ih • port) — an airport for helicopters

level (LEV • ul) — flat; even

passenger (PASS • in • jer) — a person who rides in a bus, train, car, airplane, or ship

permission (per • MISH • un) — agreement to let someone do something

pilot (PY•lut) — a person who runs an aircraft

power (POW•er) — energy

radar (RAY•dar) — something used to find the location and speed of airplanes

runway — land on which aircraft take off and land

service (SER•viss) — to supply the needs of people

speed — how fast something is going

taxi (TAKS•ee) — to move slowly on a runway in an airplane

terminal (TER•mih•nul) — a station

weapon (WEH•pun) — something used to harm someone or protect yourself

weather (WEH•thir) — how hot, cold, sunny, rainy, windy it is at a certain time

wind sock — a cloth tube attached to a pole which shows wind direction

yoke (YOHK) — something which is used to steer an airplane

INDEX

INDEX

About the Author

David Petersen started his flying career in the military service. He served in the Orient and on aircraft carriers in the Pacific. Upon leaving the service he joined the staff of a touring-motorcycle magazine, where he became managing editor. David recently moved to Durango, Colorado. He makes his living as a free-lance writer and photographer, and spends his spare time hiking and camping in the mountains. He also holds a commercial helicopter pilot's license.